Writers Uncovered

JACQUELINE WILSON

Vic Parker

Heinemann LIBRARY

www.heinemann.co.uk/library
Visit our website to find out more information about Heinemann Library books.

To order:

☎ Phone 44 (0) 1865 888066

📄 Send a fax to 44 (0) 1865 314091

🖥 Visit the Heinemann bookshop at www.heinemann.co.uk/library to browse our catalogue and order online.

First published in Great Britain by Heinemann Library, Halley Court, Jordan Hill, Oxford OX2 8EJ, part of Harcourt Education.

Heinemann is a registered trademark of Harcourt Education Ltd.

Editorial: Charlotte Guillain and Dave Harris
Design: Richard Parker and Q2A Solutions
Picture research: Hannah Taylor and Bea Ray
Production: Duncan Gilbert

Originated by Chroma Graphics (O) Pte Ltd.
Printed and bound in China by
South China Printing Company

10 digit ISBN: 0 431 90628 9
13 digit ISBN: 978 0 431 90628 7

10 09 08 07 06
10 9 8 7 6 5 4 3 2 1

British Library Cataloguing in Publication Data
Parker, Vic
    Jacqueline Wilson. – (Writers uncovered)
    823.9'14
A full catalogue record for this book is available from the British Library.

Acknowledgements
The publishers would like to thank the following for permission to reproduce photographs:
Alamy Images p. **22** (Jeff Morgan); BBC p. **26** (Giles Park); Camera Press pp. **37** (Karim Merie), **4** (Wattie Cheung); David Gordon p. **23**; Getty Images pp. **7**, **13**, **14** (Hulton Archive), **17** (Photodisc); Jacqueline Wilson pp. **6**, **8**, **9**, **12**, **16**, **20**, **24**; Kingston Historical Society p. **10**; Oxford University Press p. **18**; Penguin p. **11**; Polka Theatre p. **38**; Random House pp. **27**, **29**, **31**, **33**, **35**; Random House/Nick Sharratt pp. **19**, **21**; Rex Features pp. **42** (Phillippe Hays), **36**; Vinmag p. **15**.

Very special thanks to Jacqueline Wilson for her assistance in the preparation of this book.

Every effort has been made to contact copyright holders of any material reproduced in this book. Any omissions will be rectified in subsequent printings if notice is given to the publishers.

The paper used to print this book comes from sustainable resources.

CONTENTS

Words appearing in the text in bold, **like this**, are explained in the glossary.

Have you heard of *The Story of Tracy Beaker, Double Act,* or *The Illustrated Mum*? The chances are, they are among your favourite books. They are all written by a small, skinny, spiky-haired woman called Jacqueline Wilson, who has been described as a cross between a fairy godmother and a **gothic** granny!

Jacqueline Wilson's children's stories became the most borrowed books in public libraries in the UK in 2004. They fly off bookshop shelves at the amazing rate of 50,000 each month, giving an incredible total of over 20 million sold, so far, in the UK alone. Millions more have sold all over the world, and copies have been translated into 30 different languages. Jacqueline has won or been **shortlisted** for every major book award in Britain.

Jacqueline's face is almost as famous as her stories.

Why is Jacqueline Wilson so special?

Jacqueline Wilson's readers adore her because she understands what it is like to be a young person today. Her stories face up to serious problems such as divorce and homelessness, but are written in a chatty, familiar style. Thousands of fans flock from miles away to meet Jacqueline when she goes on visits.

Jacqueline feels just as strongly about her readers as they do about her. She is known to have spent eight hours signing books for waiting fans without a break. She always makes sure that she has a chat with everyone who has come to see her. Jacqueline treasures her millions of young readers as her huge, extended family. She is passionate about writing stories for everyone to enjoy.

FIND OUT MORE...

Here are some of Jacqueline's favourites:

Favourite food...	Fruit, cakes, chips, ice cream – but not all together at the same time!
Favourite TV show...	She does not watch much television, but she does enjoy *ER*, and her favourite children's programme has to be *The Story of Tracy Beaker*
Favourite music...	The rock group Queen
Favourite film...	An old black-and-white film called *Mandy* about a little girl who could not hear
Favourite animal...	Lemurs
Favourite colour...	Black and silver
Favourite saying...	"If life gives you lemons, make lemonade!" Which means, whatever situation you find yourself in, think positive and make the best of it.

Jacqueline was born in the ancient city of Bath, on 17 December 1945, just after the end of World War II. Her parents, Harry and Margaret Aitken, had met in the city at a dance. Harry did skilled work as a **draughtsman** and Margaret did office work for the Royal Navy.

An unsettled start

The terrible times after World War II meant that life was difficult. At first, the young family lived in a **lodging** house, where the **landlady** threatened to throw them out if baby Jacqueline's crying disturbed her. After a couple of years, Harry changed job and the family went to live with Jacqueline's grandparents in Kingston upon Thames, near bombed-out London. Sharing a house was a squash, but Jacqueline loved her grandma. She was an excellent dressmaker and she made beautiful sets of clothes for Jacqueline's dolls.

Jacqueline has fond memories of living with her grandparents.

Fitting in

Next, Jacqueline's parents moved into cramped rented rooms in a part of London called Lewisham. Jacqueline started school, but she did not settle in well. She had to have a lot of time off sick, and she also hated school dinners. Then the family were given a council flat, back in Kingston upon Thames. Jacqueline was thrilled to have her own room for the first time. She also liked her new school, Latchmere Primary.

FIND OUT MORE...

In World War II (1939–1945), many nations, including Britain, France, Russia, and the United States, fought against Germany, Japan, and Italy. Over 45 million people were killed and millions more were injured. Cities all over Europe were reduced to rubble, and there were shortages of homes, food and supplies which lasted for many years after the war ended.

During World War II, many buildings in London and other cities were completely destroyed by German bombs.

Let's pretend

Jacqueline's favourite teacher was Mr Townsend, because he encouraged his class to use their imaginations. "Making believe" is what Jacqueline did best. On her way to school, she made up stories in her head. Each break-time, she invented imaginary games to play. At lunchtimes, she and her friends sometimes hid in a room filled with play costumes and dressed up as different characters.

Jacqueline in her Latchmere school uniform.

INSIDE INFORMATION

Jacqueline has always felt deeply for children who have a tough life. At her school, one girl was dreadfully teased for being overweight. Another boy was mocked for being brainy – by one of the teachers! One girl even had to deal with her mother dying from cancer. The characters in Jacqueline's stories often have to get through upsetting circumstances like these.

Only but not lonely

Jacqueline was always on her own after school, before her parents returned from work. But she loved having time to herself to play with her dolls. Jacqueline invented names and personalities for them all, and dreamed up endless stories about each one.

Jacqueline and her parents on a rare day out all together.

Time with Mum and Dad

Jacqueline's parents often argued, so they usually did things with Jacqueline separately. Jacqueline's mother helped her find interesting dolls and collect photographs of her favourite movie star, Mandy Miller. Jacqueline's father sometimes took her walking in the countryside or joined in her imaginary games. He also read to Jacqueline and occasionally bought home books for her, because she adored stories.

Story time

Jacqueline could spend literally hours tucked away in a quiet corner, reading. She often read a book a day, and went on endless book-swapping trips to the library. When she worked her way through the children's section, her mother got her early membership of the adult section. Jacqueline found it very frustrating when the books she wanted were not there.

Jacqueline decided that borrowing books was good, but owning books was even better. She always asked for books as birthday and Christmas presents. On holiday, as a special treat, Jacqueline's mum and dad would take her to a second-hand bookshop to choose a story or two. In this way Jacqueline began creating a library of her own.

The library in Kingston upon Thames is still one of Jacqueline's favourite places today.

Putting pen to paper

As well as reading books, Jacqueline loved making her own. She used fancy pens to fill hundreds of bright, shiny notebooks with stories. Sometimes Jacqueline would copy illustrations from her favourite books and invent new stories around them. Jacqueline also liked to cut out pictures of models from sewing pattern catalogues. She stuck the characters down in her notebooks and used these as inspiration for stories.

Jacqueline especially loved to copy Eve Garnett's illustrations from the story *The Family from One End Street*.

A firm friend

At the age of eleven, Jacqueline went to Coombe Girls' School in New Malden, Surrey. She made a friend on her first day there, Chris, who she still sees to this day. The two girls shared lots of fun times going to each other's houses for tea, having sleepovers, eyeing up boys at the local swimming pool, window-shopping, and going to dance halls and jazz clubs.

Jacqueline and a friend in their Coombe school uniforms.

Must try harder!

Jacqueline did not do as well as she could have at school, because she put all the effort that she should have put into homework into writing stories. By fifteen, she had written a full-length novel! Jacqueline was good at English, History and Art, but dreadful at Maths and Science. She left school at sixteen, after passing six **'O' level** exams. She would have liked to continue studying English, but nobody explained that she could go to a College of Further Education. Instead, Jacqueline was expected to find a job. She dreamed of being a writer in the same way that other teenagers dreamed of being a movie star or a famous singer. She never thought that her dream could come true.

FIND OUT MORE...

Jacqueline was a teenager in the late 1950s and early 1960s. There were lots of exciting ideas around then, from new hairstyles to rock 'n' roll music. For the first time ever, teenagers had their own fashions and **idols**, such James Dean and Elvis Presley. It was a great time to be a young person growing up.

Rock 'n' roll dancing was a big craze when Jacqueline was a teenager in the 1950s.

In 1961, when Jacqueline left school, there were only a few types of work considered suitable for girls – mainly shop work, office work, nursing or teaching. Jacqueline's parents encouraged her to sign up for a year's secretarial course. Jacqueline never really wanted to be a secretary. By a stroke of luck, she was looking through a newspaper one day when she spotted an advert for teenage writers. It had been placed by a magazine company called DC Thomson, who wanted to launch a magazine for teenage girls. Jacqueline sent in a short, funny story about going to a disco and being the only girl not asked to dance. To her amazement, the company bought it… then bought several more of her stories… then offered her a job!

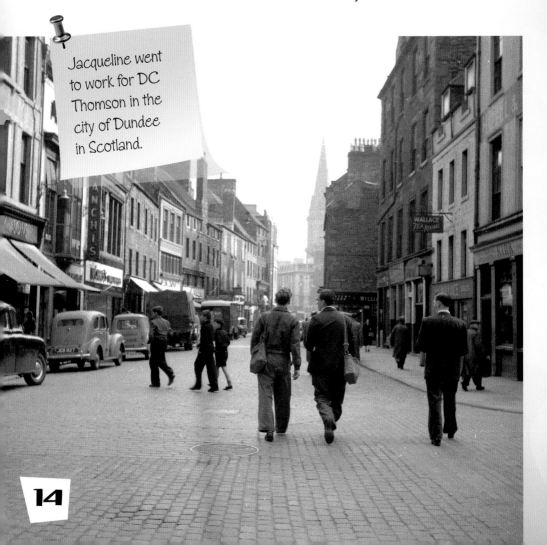

Jacqueline went to work for DC Thomson in the city of Dundee in Scotland.

Living away from home

The magazine company's offices were in Dundee, Scotland. This meant Jacqueline had to move hundreds of miles from home. She stayed in a Church of Scotland hostel. The magazine company published popular boys' comics, such as the *Beano* and the *Dandy*, and bestselling women's magazines. Jacqueline wrote stories and articles for the women's magazines, including making up the star signs and readers' letters! She wrote for the company's new teenage girls' magazine too, which was called *Jackie* after her.

Jackie became the best-selling magazine for teenage girls.

February 8, 1964. Every Thursday 6d

Jackie
for go-ahead teens

FOUR MORE PIN-UPS FOR YOUR COLLECTION. BIG SIZE. TRUE-LIFE COLOUR.

RINGO TELLS HOW THE BEATLE CUT BEGAN—see Pete Lennon's page.

SCARVES ARE EYE-CATCHING —AND BOY-CATCHING. LATEST IN GIMMICK-WEAR in colour on pages 18 and 19.

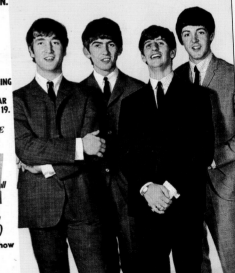

INSIDE INFORMATION

Working for the magazine company taught Jacqueline to be disciplined about writing. She always had a fixed number of words to write, on a set subject, by a certain time. There was no room for excuses or for not meeting the deadline! This is why today, Jacqueline never suffers from **writer's block.**

A girl in love

It was not long before Jacqueline met a young man called Millar Wilson. They fell in love and in 1965 they got married. The couple decided to move back to Kingston upon Thames and Millar joined the police force. Jacqueline continued to write magazine articles from home. She also wrote novels for adults, but to her dismay, book publishing companies turned them down. Still, Jacqueline never thought of giving up. Writing was something she loved doing too much to stop.

A new arrival

In 1967, Jacqueline gave birth to a beautiful baby daughter, Emma. She was overjoyed to be a mum, but still kept up her writing. While little Emma was asleep, playing, or at a morning nursery session, Jacqueline worked fast. She wrote at least 10,000 words a week for magazines, besides always having a novel in progress.

Jacqueline, Millar and their daughter Emma were a happy young family.

HAVE A GO

Jacqueline's top tip for aspiring writers is to keep a diary, like many of the characters in her stories. Jotting down the everyday story of your life is a brilliant way to make sure that you get into the habit of writing on a regular basis. You can scribble in any ideas you have for other stories too, so you do not forget them.

But Jacqueline warns that if you have got a nosy family, you had better find somewhere safe to hide your diary!

Jacqueline's first book

As a young mother, stuck at home and without much money, Jacqueline often spent her spare time at the library. She searched out good stories to read to Emma.

Emma was a toddler when Jacqueline discovered a series of children's books called Nippers. They appealed to her because they were modern tales about inner-city children – just the type of children's story that Jacqueline thought that she would like to write. She had a go at one called *Ricky's Birthday*, and sent it to the company, Macmillan, who produced the Nippers books. To her delight, it was accepted. Jacqueline was finally going to see her name on the cover of a book!

17

Jacqueline did not become hugely successful very quickly. In fact, after choosing to publish *Ricky's Birthday*, Macmillan rejected the next story she wrote for their Nippers series. Despite this, Jacqueline was already working hard on another novel for adults. It was about two girls who get kidnapped, and it was called *Hide and Seek*.

Macmillan thought that Jacqueline's new story was just right to fit in with their adult crime books. Jacqueline wrote four more similar stories. Even though they were written for adults, these books all had children as central characters. Jacqueline knew that she did not really want to write for adults at all. She wanted to write for young people.

Novels for teenagers

Around ten years after Jacqueline had written *Ricky's Birthday*, she wrote a novel for teenagers called *Nobody's Perfect*. Jacqueline was very pleased with it, but to her disappointment it was turned down by several publishers. Finally, Oxford University Press offered to publish the book.

The front cover of Jacqueline's first novel for teenagers.

18

Jacqueline wrote several more stories for young people. The books all focused on girls of around fifteen years old. They were dark, thought-provoking stories with plots that covered **controversial** subjects that teenagers wanted to read about, such as suicide, sex, and witchcraft.

The perfect partnership

Jacqueline's **editor** moved to another publishing company, called Transworld. He suggested that Jacqueline might like to write for this company too, but for a younger age group. It was good timing – Jacqueline already had the idea for a funny, but moving, story for younger children. It was going to be about a child in care who wanted to be fostered, and it would be called *The Story of Tracy Beaker*.

Jacqueline wanted *The Story of Tracy Beaker* to be illustrated, like her own favourite books from her childhood. Her editor suggested an artist called Nick Sharratt. He drew illustrations which looked as if they had been done by the child who was telling the story. Jacqueline was delighted. She was also pleased with the way Nick's drawings broke up the text. She thought this made her story look inviting for children who did not usually like reading books.

Nick Sharratt's drawings brought Jacqueline's characters to life.

A breakthrough book

When *The Story of Tracy Beaker* was published in 1991, it was a huge success. Young readers loved it, and critics praised it too. The book was shortlisted for two top awards – the Smarties Prize and the Carnegie Medal. Suddenly, Jacqueline was not just an author any more. She was now a famous, best-selling author.

Jacqueline and Nick Sharratt are a winning combination.

Jacqueline's success story

Since then, Jacqueline has had over 80 books for children published. Some are for very young children, such as *The Monster Story Teller* and *My Brother Bernadette*. Most of her books are for readers aged eight and over, such as *Vicky Angel*, *Dustbin Baby*, *Lola Rose*, and the *Girls* series. These books are always illustrated with Nick Sharratt's fantastic drawings. They deal with serious issues such as divorce, illness, and death, and also strong emotions such as hatred, loneliness, and jealousy. However, Jacqueline ensures that her stories always make readers laugh as well as cry.

One of Nick's drawings from *The Illustrated Mum*.

FIND OUT MORE...

Jacqueline's favourite of all her own stories is *The Illustrated Mum*. She has many other favourite children's books. Today, Jacqueline especially enjoys the work of other contemporary authors, such as *Make Lemonade* by Virginia Ewer Woolf, *Out of the Dust* by Karen Hesse, and *The Midwife's Apprentice* and *Catherine, Called Birdy* by Karen Cushman.

Her best-loved teenage reads were often classics such as the novels of Jane Austen and Charlotte Brontë, as well as *Gone with the Wind*, and *The Diary of Anne Frank*. As a child, she liked stories about large families, such as *Little Women* by Louisa M Alcott, and tales with adventurous heroines, such as *Nancy and Plum* by Betty Macdonald.

Being Jacqueline Wilson

Today, as a best-selling, world-famous author, Jacqueline is kept extremely busy meeting her readers at schools, libraries and bookshops, giving interviews and talks, and attending business meetings. Whether she is out and about or at home writing, Jacqueline always tries to swim 50 lengths of her local swimming pool first thing in the morning, because it makes her feel good and gives her time to think.

Jacqueline often rounds off the day by opening her fanmail while watching the television. She does her best to reply to all her readers, but it is impossible, because she receives 200 to 300 letters a week! Jacqueline also likes to do something in the evenings, such as dancing, a pub quiz, the cinema, or theatre. She always reads for an hour or so before switching off the light.

Jacqueline meets fans and signs books at the Hay on Wye literary festival.

Books and dolls are among Jacqueline's favourite things.

Jacqueline's family

Jacqueline still lives in Kingston upon Thames. She lives on her own because she and Millar have divorced. Her elderly mum lives nearby. Her daughter Emma is grown-up and lives in Cambridge, where she teaches French at the university and writes books for students. Jacqueline and Emma talk every day on the phone, and sometimes they go on holiday together.

FIND OUT MORE...

Jacqueline likes to collect things, such as the silver rings she wears on her fingers. She buys a new ring every time she has a book published. Jacqueline owns over 15,000 books, a huge collection of dolls and toys, lots of pictures, and an assortment of strange things such as a full-sized fashion dummy. Her house is **Victorian**, because another one of her obsessions is the Victorian era.

JACQUELINE'S WORK

Jacqueline makes sure she writes every day, no matter where she is or what she is doing. She still uses fancy pens and pretty exercise books, just as she did when she was little. If she is at home, she will write about 1,000 words a day sitting comfortably at her desk. If she has got to travel somewhere, she goes by train so she can work on the journey. When Jacqueline is happy with what she has written, she types it up on a computer. She has a laptop, but she cannot take it about from place to place because if she unplugged it from all of its equipment, she would not know how to wire it all back up again.

For many years, Jacqueline used to type up her finished work on a trusty old typewriter.

Ideas and inspiration

When she is writing about young people, Jacqueline does not think back to when she was young. Instead, she imagines what it is like to be young now. Jacqueline dreams up a character and wonders about their personality and their life. This gives her ideas for starting a story.

Jacqueline's characters often face difficult situations, such as fitting into a step-family, being homeless, or being bullied. But she never sets out deliberately to explore a particular issue. Jacqueline begins writing as soon as she has got to know a character vividly in her head. Then she discovers the problems the character has to face and how their story unfolds as she goes along.

INSIDE INFORMATION

When she started writing for adults, Jacqueline was inspired to write crime novels by her interest in her husband Millar's police work. In Jacqueline's later book for young people called *Midnight*, the character Violet's dad is a policeman. But when he talks about his work, Violet finds it really boring!

HAVE A GO

Jacqueline writes her stories in the first person. This means that she writes using "I" (for example "I couldn't believe it!"). This allows her to tell things from a child's point of view, in a child's voice. Writing as "he" or "she" is called writing in the third person. Try writing a story about a character either in the first or third person. If you write in the first person, imagine you are in the situation yourself. If you use the third person, imagine you are watching what is happening.

THE STORY OF TRACY BEAKER

The plot

Tracy Beaker has been in care for almost as long as she can remember – but she's sure her mum will zoom up in her sports car with presents and hugs and kisses, and rescue her sometime soon. In the meantime, Tracy's set her sights on getting herself out of the "Stowey House Dumping Ground for Difficult Kids" by being fostered. Unfortunately, it is proving rather troublesome to identify potential takers – until, that is, an unsuspecting writer called Cam pays a visit.

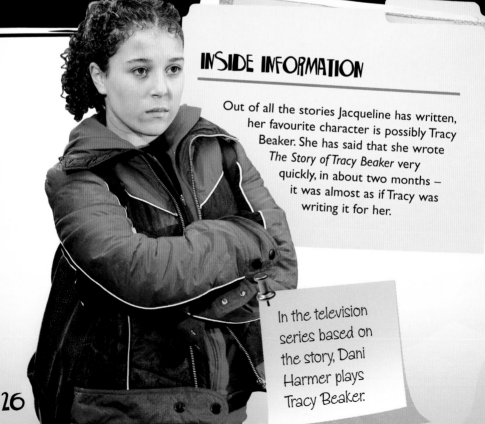

INSIDE INFORMATION

Out of all the stories Jacqueline has written, her favourite character is possibly Tracy Beaker. She has said that she wrote *The Story of Tracy Beaker* very quickly, in about two months – it was almost as if Tracy was writing it for her.

In the television series based on the story, Dani Harmer plays Tracy Beaker.

A major theme: Imagination

Tracy relies on her huge imagination to help her deal with difficult situations and strong feelings, like hurt, jealousy and anger. For instance, she imagines being a witch and "zapping" Louise so all her golden curls fall out. She also invents endless excuses why her mother has not come to get her, such as she's too busy being a glamorous movie star in Hollywood.

Tracy keeps her spirits up by dreaming about what her life will be like in the future. For example, in one fantasy, she pictures herself having so much money that she can afford to have her own house, to employ someone to foster her, and to eat a birthday cake all to herself every day. But will Tracy be able to turn any of these wonderful dreams into reality?

The Story of Tracy Beaker was published in 1991.

THE SUITCASE KID

The plot

Andy West's parents are getting divorced, and she can't choose whether to live with her mum or her dad. She ends up being shuttled back and forth between them both. Living out of a suitcase is bad, but trying to fit into two new families is worse. Thankfully, Andy has her lucky **mascot** rabbit, Radish, for comfort. All they want is for everything to go back to how it used to be…

A major theme: Loss

Andy has to deal with the loss of everything she loved about her life. Andy has lost being part of a small, close family, an only child with two loving parents. Andy has lost her cosy family home, Mulberry Cottage. Andy has lost her privacy – at her mum's new home, Andy has to share a bedroom with her stepsister Katie, and at her dad's new home, Andy has to share a bedroom with her twin stepsister and stepbrother. The only time Andy manages to find space is when she locks herself into the bathroom for a while! Along with losing her space, Andy has lost her possessions. All her special things, like her beloved books, have been packed up and stored somewhere. The only thing Andy feels she has left is Radish, but then she thinks she has lost her as well.

Andy has to face the fact that things cannot go back to how they were. However, Andy discovers that she is not the only person in this sort of situation. Katie seems spoilt and nasty, but she has had hidden fears and problems since her mother died.

The Suitcase Kid was published a year after The Story of Tracy Beaker, in 1992.

INSIDE INFORMATION

Radish is actually Jacqueline's own lucky mascot rabbit. Jacqueline always has Radish close at hand while she is writing. She likes playing games with Radish too. Her favourite is Bunny Bungee. Jacqueline uses a rubber band to tie her to a strong pencil, then Radish dives over the edge of the desk!

Andy also finds special new things ease the pain of what she has lost: a new friend in her stepbrother Graham, a new grandparent-type relationship with an old couple called Mr and Mrs Peters, her own private space in the Peters' magical garden, and even a new baby sister.

THE BED AND BREAKFAST STAR

The plot

When Elsa's stepdad cannot find work, her family cannot afford to stay in their cosy home, and they face life on the streets. The only accommodation the council can offer them is bed-and-breakfast at the Royal Hotel – but the Royal Hotel is far from being the palace it sounds. Elsa makes the most of her dingy surroundings while she **fantasizes** about being a big name on TV one day. Elsa never dreams that a disaster at the Royal Hotel might allow her to shine as a real star.

A major theme: Poverty

Like all the families at the Royal Hotel, Elsa's family is very poor. Her mum and stepdad struggle to cope with their desperate circumstances. Plunged into **depression**, they cannot face getting up in the morning and lie in bed until mid-day. Elsa helps her mum by looking after her little sister Pippa, but she still often finds her mum crying and even Elsa's best jokes fail to cheer her up. Elsa's stepdad, Mack, feels he has failed the family. He has given up on trying to find work and blows what little money the family has.

Elsa hates school because everyone labels her "bed-and-breakfast" – not just the other children, but even the teachers! Not only does this make Elsa stick out, it also means that everyone sees her as a certain type of person and no one encourages her potential as an individual.

However, Elsa uses every method she can think of to stay cheerful. For instance, when there is hardly any food on offer for breakfast, she makes herself a tasty sugar sandwich. She even sometimes tells herself her own jokes.

Elsa shows that people can refuse to let their lives be defined by their circumstances. She refuses to disappear quietly with all the other "problem" families that society wants to get rid of. She has a loud voice and is not afraid to use its full force to be heard. In the end, she forces everybody to take notice of what a brave, determined person she truly is.

The Bed and Breakfast Star was published in 1994.

INSIDE INFORMATION

Whenever the going gets tough, Elsa tells jokes to cheer everyone up. Jacqueline thinks that humour is an excellent way of dealing with sad or worrying things. She is a firm believer in thinking positive and that you can always bounce back!

DOUBLE ACT

The plot

Everything about twins Ruby and Garnet is identical – except for their personalities. Ruby is outgoing, while Garnet is shy. Ruby likes being the centre of attention, while Garnet hates being in the spotlight.

Since their mother died, the twins have banded together against the world. But everything is about to change. The twins' dad is moving the family to a new life in the countryside. Gran is staying behind, but their dad's new girlfriend, Rose, is coming with them. When each twin starts to cope with the changes in their own separate way, their lifelong double act begins to crumble.

A major theme: Individuality

Sometimes it can be difficult to know who you really are, to find the right direction for your life and follow it. Garnet hides behind Ruby and finds confidence in doing everything together. She admits that she likes everyone thinking of them not as individual people, but as "the Twins". Ruby likes this too, but for different reasons – it helps Ruby stand out from the crowd and be noticed!

It is tough for both girls to realise that they are holding each other back. How will they work out what they want for the future? Other characters in the story have to go through similar decision-making. The twins' dad chooses to leave a safe, familiar job he hates and risks making a new career based on a hobby he loves – collecting secondhand books. Even Gran chooses her own path – she decides to live in **sheltered accommodation** and make her own life away from the family. Decisions like these make the twins feel upset and angry. In contrast, Rose is a selfless character, supporting both her boyfriend and each twin when they discover their individual ambitions.

Jacqueline's story shows that you have to follow your own heart, but that you also have to allow other people to do the same, in order to find true happiness.

INSIDE INFORMATION

In *Double Act* Jacqueline writes as though she is both Ruby and Garnet. Outspoken Ruby's voice is printed in bold, **like this**, and shy Garnet's voice is printed in more subtle italics, *like this*.

Double Act
Jacqueline Wilson
WINNER OF THE SMARTIES BOOK PRIZE
WINNER OF THE CHILDREN'S BOOK AWARD

Double Act has two illustrators: Nick Sharratt drew all the pictures of Ruby, and Sue Heap drew all the pictures of Garnet. The story was published in 1995.

THE ILLUSTRATED MUM

The plot

Marigold is not like the other mothers at the school gates. She is covered from head to toe with unique **tattoos** and wears outrageous clothes. She also has extraordinary ideas, such as feeding her daughters on just cake or ice cream, or buying 1950s glittery dancing sandals for Dolphin instead of sensible school shoes. However, the biggest difference is that Marigold suffers from severe mental illness. Dolphin and Star are worn out with looking after her. When an opportunity arrives for the girls to leave, the desperate Star strikes out on her own, but Dolphin cannot bring herself to abandon Marigold. She is determined to stay and help her mother – but when Marigold's problems become too big for Dolphin to handle, who will help Dolphin?

A major theme: Responsibility

Because of their mother's mental illness, Dolphin and Star are weighed down with grown-up responsibilities. They not only have to look after themselves on their own at home, they also have to take care of the grown-up who should be responsible for them – their mother.

There are very few responsible adult characters in *The Illustrated Mum*. Most of the teachers at Dolphin's school show no understanding of Dolphin's problematic home life; Dolphin and Star's **landlady** continually criticises and threatens the girls instead of offering any help; and the mother of Dolphin's friend, Oliver, is weak and unable to help. When Star's father appears on the scene, he offers to take on responsibility for the two girls, but wants nothing to do with their sick mother. He also does this in a very irresponsible way, offering the girls a home behind their mother's back and without involving any of the **authorities**. His actions only plunge the girls into a new set of problems. Instead, the young people have to take on the responsibility of sorting out their grown-up issues in a grown-up world.

INSIDE INFORMATION

Jacqueline has said: "Sometimes I upset adult readers because I write from the child's point of view about parents who let them down – I can see that that might be unsettling". However, most adults think that Jacqueline's stories are very helpful for children, because they face up bravely to the problems of real modern-day life.

The Illustrated Mum deals with very serious issues, but manages to be very entertaining at the same time. It was published in 1999.

PRIZES, PERFORMANCES, AND PRAISE

The Story of Tracy Beaker won the People's Choice Award from television programme *Blue Peter*. This was special for Jacqueline because it came from her readers. Since then, Jacqueline has won or been shortlisted for over 30 major awards from the book publishing industry. These include:

- winning the Children's Book Award for *The Suitcase Kid* and *Double Act*
- winning the Smarties Book Prize for *Double Act* and *Lizzie Zipmouth*
- winning the Guardian Children's Fiction Prize and the British Book Awards Children's Book of the Year for *The Illustrated Mum*
- being shortlisted for the Carnegie Medal for *Double Act*, *The Bed and Breakfast Star*, *Bad Girls*, *The Illustrated Mum* and *The Story of Tracy Beaker*.
- being shortlisted for the Whitbread Children's Book Award, for *The Illustrated Mum*.

Jacqueline has attended lots of award ceremonies – and been a winner at many of them!

Here is Jacqueline at the Childline awards with TV presenter Esther Rantzen and the Countess of Wessex.

Special honours

In 2002, the Queen chose Jacqueline for an award called the Officer of the Order of the British Empire, which means that Jacqueline now has letters after her name: Jacqueline Wilson OBE. Jacqueline went to Buckingham Palace to receive her OBE from the Queen in person.

In 2004, the Queen invited Jacqueline there again, to attend a special lunch for women who have reached the top in their line of work. Jacqueline was picked because of her best-selling writing, along with other high-achieving women. In the same year, the children's charity, Childline, gave Jacqueline a special award to recognise how she helps thousands of children by writing about the difficult situations they face in their lives. The Chair of the charity, Esther Rantzen, said: "She is truly a hero to so many children."

Curtain up

In 1999, Jacqueline was delighted when the famous Polka Theatre for Children, in Wimbledon, London, turned her story *The Lottie Project* into a play. She liked it so much that she went to see it three times! Since then, *Double Act*, *Bad Girls* and *Midnight* have been adapted for the stage too. The plays sometimes tour around the country, so look out for performances at a theatre near you.

Jacqueline loves to see her stories brought to life on stage, in performances such as this version of *The Lottie Project*.

Over the airwaves

Jacqueline has loved hearing adaptations of *The Bed and Breakfast Star*, *The Story of Tracy Beaker* and *The Dare Game* broadcast on BBC Radio 4. Several of her stories have also been turned into major dramas on the main television channels. The BBC's *Tracy Beaker* has become the all-time favourite programme of many seven- to eleven-year-olds.

The versions of Jacqueline's stories that appear on stage or are broadcast on television are written by specialists called scriptwriters. How would you go about turning your favourite Jacqueline Wilson book into a play or devising an episode of CBBC's *Tracy Beaker*? If you want to try writing a script, here are some things to think about:

- How will you tell your audience what your characters are thinking and feeling inside? You can do this entirely through your characters' dialogue and action, or you could have a character who occasionally speaks directly to the audience, or a **narrator**.
- How will you handle the timescale of your story? A play usually starts at the beginning of a story and works its way through to the end – but you can have "flashback" scenes of the past or "dream" scenes of the future.
- Try to break your action up into scenes that take place in different settings – but do not have too many if you are writing a play for the stage or you will need too much scenery!
- Try to make your characters' speech realistic.
- You can include brief instructions to the actors in your script too, to tell them how you want them to speak their lines (for instance, "angrily") and what they should be doing (such as, "she stomps upstairs").
- You could also suggest some special effects, such as stunts, or music.

Views in the news

When you are a famous author like Jacqueline, people called critics write their opinions of your work for newspapers and magazines. These are known as book reviews, and they help readers decide whether to spend their time and money on a story or not. Here is an example of a review for *Midnight*, with some notes on how the critic has put it together. Would it encourage you to read the book?

Midnight is another unforgettable tale about growing up in a modern family from best-selling writer Jacqueline Wilson, author of *The Story of Tracy Beaker*.

Readers of ten and over will be moved by the lonely life of thirteen-year-old Violet, trapped under the sinister influence of her controlling older brother, Will. Violet escapes from reality by reading the fairy stories of Casper Dream. She writes many confiding fanletters to the author she adores – although she never has the confidence to send them! Everything brightens when the exciting new girl at school, Jasmine, becomes Violet's friend. But when Violet's new-found happiness crumbles, can her favourite author and his magical world help her?

Midnight has all the qualities of Wilson's previous successes: brilliant characterisation; realistic and complex relationships, situations and emotions; an effortless writing style. However, it is more subtle than many of her best-loved stories, which have a strong thread of humour woven into them.

This spell-binding book will delight people who enjoy sensitive stories about friendship and adoration, mystery and dreams, and is a must-read for all Jacqueline Wilson fans.

a summary of what kind of book it is

some background on the author

who the book is aimed at

a little about the the story, without giving too much away

the critic's opinion on whether it is a good or bad read, with clear reasons

comparison with other books

a recommendation of who the critic thinks will like the book

HAVE A GO

Why not try writing your own review of a Jacqueline Wilson book? You could give it to a friend who does not know the story and see if they go on to read it. Ask them to write a review back, recommending one of their own favourite books to you. You might discover a great new book or author.

Pieces of praise

Here are some critics' opinions about Jacqueline's work:

"Wilson writes like a child... The tone of voice is faultless, her stories are about the problems many children face, and her plots work with classic simplicity... A subtle art is concealed by artlessness, and some might call that genius..."

The Daily Telegraph

"It takes courage and honesty to explore what can be emotionally scary areas."

Anne Brogan, executive producer of the TV series Girls in Love

"Her appeal is extraordinary, and I think it's due to the fact that she writes directly – never down. She taps into something that young girls especially, but certainly boys too, recognise as being distinctively like themselves."

Top writer, Philip Pullman

LONG LIVE JACQUELINE WILSON!

It takes Jacqueline roughly six months to write a book from start to finish. So there are about two new Jacqueline Wilson stories published per year. But today, Jacqueline Wilson fans do not just want her books, they want Jacqueline Wilson everything. Manufacturers are creating writing kits, greeting cards, games, sweets, and all sorts of fashionable accessories to keep up with the demand.

Future plans

Jacqueline has plenty of ideas for other stories. She says that to stop writing would be like stopping cleaning her teeth! Jacqueline will also continue to travel up and down the country and go abroad on book tours, because she says that meeting her readers is one of the things she enjoys best about being a successful writer. Who knows, you might meet her yourself one day.

Jacqueline has signed literally thousands of books for her fans.

Writing in focus

Jacqueline has millions of fans worldwide. Here is what some of them think about her and her work:

"I love Jacqueline Wilson and all my friends do too."
Aisling, age 11, from Northern Ireland

"Thank you, Jacqueline Wilson, for writing about what it's like to be me."
Sara, age 10, from Boston, USA

"The only way Jacqueline Wilson could improve on her stories is if she wrote more words, so they lasted longer, or if she wrote faster, so there were more of them!"
Aya, age 12, from Lebanon

JACQUELINE'S WISH LIST

Hopes...   As a child, Jacqueline always longed for a dog – but she could not have one because they were not allowed in council flats. If her life ever quietens down, Jacqueline would love a small dog, such as a Yorkshire Terrier or a miniature poodle.

Dreams...   If Jacqueline could meet anyone who has ever been famous, she would choose:
1) the late Freddie Mercury, lead singer of the rock band Queen;
2) Louisa M Alcott, the author of Little Women;
3) David Hockney, the modern-day artist.

Ambitions...   Jacqueline is content with her life and her achievements. She would just like to keep doing what she is doing for as long as possible. But she says it would be nice to have 100 published books, and to win a dancing competition!

TIMELINE

1945 Jacqueline Aitken is born on December 17.

1950 Jacqueline goes to Latchmere Primary School.

1956 Jacqueline goes to Coombe Girls Secondary School.

1961 Jacqueline leaves school and does a year's secretarial course.

1962 Jacqueline goes to work for magazine company DC Thomson in Dundee, Scotland, as a writer.

1965 Jacqueline marries Millar Wilson.

1966 Jacqueline moves back to her home town, Kingston upon Thames, with Millar.

1967 Jacqueline and Millar's daughter, Emma, is born.

1973 Jacqueline has a children's story published, called *Ricky's Birthday*.

1973–1980 Jacqueline has several crime novels for adults published.

1982 Jacqueline has a novel for teenagers published, *Nobody's Perfect*.

1983–1990 Jacqueline has more books for young people published, including *Waiting for the Sky to Fall*, *The School Trip*, *The Other Side*, *Amber*, *Lonely Hearts*, *Supersleuth*, *The Power of the Shade*, *This Girl*, *Vampire*, *Falling Apart*, *Is There Anybody There?*, *The Left Outs*, *The Party in the Lift*, and *Take a Good Look*.

1991 *The Story of Tracy Beaker* is published, illustrated by Nick Sharatt. *The Dream Palace* and *The Werepuppy* are published.

1992 *The Suitcase Kid* is published and wins the Children's Book Award both this year and the next.
Mark Spark and *Video Rose* are published.

1993 *Deep Blue*, *Mark Spark in the Dark*, and *The Mum-minder* are published.

1994 *The Bed and Breakfast Star*, *Come Back, Teddy!*, *Freddy's Teddy*, *Teddy at the Fair*, *Teddy Goes Swimming*, *The Werepuppy on Holiday*, and *Twin Trouble* are published.

1995 *Double Act* is published and is shortlisted for the Carnegie Medal. and the Writers' Guild Award for Best Children's Book. It wins the Nestlé Smarties Book Prize (Gold Award).
The Bed and Breakfast Star is shortlisted for the Carnegie Medal. It wins the Young Telegraph/Fully Booked Award.
Cliffhanger, *Jimmy Jelly*, *Love from Katie*, *My Brother Bernadette*, *Sophie's Secret Diary*, and *The Dinosaur's Packed Lunch* are published.

1996 *Bad Girls* is published and is shortlisted for the Carnegie Medal. *Beauty and the Beast, Connie and the WaterBabies,* and *Mr Cool* are published.
Double Act wins the Children's Book Award and the Sheffield Children's Book Award. It is shortlisted for the Young Telegraph/Fully Booked Award.

1997 *Girls in Love, The Lottie Project,* and *The Monster Story-Teller* are published.

1998 *The Lottie Project* is shortlisted for the Children's Book Award. *Girls Under Pressure, Buried Alive!,* and *Rapunzel* are published.

1999 *The Illustrated Mum* is published and shortlisted for both the Carnegie Medal and the Whitbread Children's Book Award.
Girls Under Pressure is shortlisted for the Children's Book Award.
Girls Out Late and *Monster Eyeballs* are published.
The Lottie Project is the first of Jacqueline's stories to be turned into a play, by the Polka Theatre for Children.

2000 *The Illustrated Mum* wins the British Book Awards Children's Book of the Year and the Guardian Children's Fiction Prize. It is shortlisted for the Children's Book Award.
Lizzie Zipmouth is published and wins the Nestlé Smarties Book Prize (Gold Award) and the Kids' Club Network Special Award.
The Dare Game and *Vicky Angel* are published.

2001 *Dustbin Baby, Sleep-overs,* and *The Cat Mummy* are published.

2002 The Queen awards Jacqueline an OBE.
The Story of Tracy Beaker is made into a children's television series.
Dustbin Baby wins the WH Smith Award for Children's Literature.
The Worry Website, Girls in Tears, and *Secrets* are published.

2003 *Lola Rose* and *Midnight* are published.
Jacqueline is shortlisted for the British Book Awards Author of the Year. *Girls in Tears* wins the British Book Awards Children's Book of the Year.

2004 Jacqueline becomes the most-borrowed author in libraries across the UK.
The Diamond Girls and *Best Friends* are published

2005 *Best Friends* wins the Red House Children's Book Award.
Love Lessons, The World of Jacqueline Wilson, and *The Jacqueline Wilson Quiz Book* are published.

FURTHER RESOURCES

More books to read

An Interview With Jacqueline Wilson, Joanna Carey (Mammoth, 2000)
The Jacqueline Wilson Quiz Book (Corgi Yearling Books, 2005)
The World of Jacqueline Wilson (Doubleday, 2005)

Audiobooks

Many of Jacqueline's stories are available as BBC audiobooks on CD and cassette, including:

The Story of Tracy Beaker (complete and unabridged), (BBC Audiobooks, 2002)

Websites

Jacqueline's official site contains lots of information, and you can join her fan club:
www.jacquelinewilson.co.uk

The BBC's Tracy Beaker website:
www.bbc.co.uk/cbbc/tracybeaker

The *Totally Tracy Beaker* magazine's website:
www.totallytracybeaker.com

If you are affected by any of the issues in Jacqueline's stories, such as bullying or divorce, you can contact ChildLine to talk about your worries in secret. Their website is:
www.childline.org.uk
(you can call them free on 0800 1111 at any time of the day or night)

Disclaimer

All the internet addresses (URLs) given in this book were valid at the time of going to press. However, due to the dynamic nature of the Internet, some addresses may have changed, or sites may have ceased to exist since publication. While the author and publishers regret any inconvenience this may cause readers, no responsibility for any such changes can be accepted by either the author or the publishers.

GLOSSARY

authorities   organizations who have power and control, such as the government

controversial   something that people have different, and strong, opinions about

depression   mental state of being seriously unhappy and unmotivated all the time, which needs medical help

draughtsman   person who draws detailed technical plans

editor   person in a publishing company who oversees the words of a book

fantasy   imaginary situation or daydream

gothic   gothic fashion mixes black clothing with big, striking pieces of jewellery

idol   someone who is admired or adored, such as a singer or film star

landlady   woman who owns a house and allows people to stay in return for paying rent

lodging   place someone lives in but does not own

mascot   object, often an animal or toy, that is believed to bring good luck

mental illness   difficulty in the way someone thinks that stops them being able to live normally, which needs medical help

narrator   person who tells a story

'O' level   exam that is equivalent to a modern GCSE

sheltered accommodation   special flats, usually for elderly people, where people can live on their own but can call for help when they need it

shortlist   final list of candidates for an award, from which the winner is selected

subtle   something that is not easily noticed but was meant to be there

tattoo   permanent design put on the body by pricking the skin with a needle and marking it with dyes

theme   idea explored in detail by an author

Victorian   something that dates back to the reign of the British Queen Victoria, 1837–1901

writer's block   problem some writers have when they are unable to think of what to write

INDEX

Titles in the *Writers Uncovered* series include:

Hardback   0 431 90626 2

Hardback   0 431 90627 0

Hardback   0 431 90628 9

Hardback   0 431 90629 7

Hardback   0 431 90630 0

Hardback   0 431 90631 9

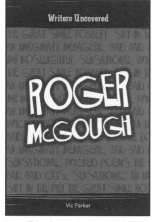

Hardback   0 431 90632 7

Hardback   0 431 90633 5

Find out about other titles from Heinemann Library on our website www.heinemann.co.uk/library